Amazing Snakes Facts

Fun Facts about Snakes
Guaranteed to Blow Your Mind

MENTAL BOMB PUBLISHING

INTRODUCTION

Whether you're a nature enthusiast, a curious explorer, or a snake aficionado, this book is your ultimate passport to understanding and appreciating the intriguing world of snakes.

This fascinating book contains hundreds of fun facts and loads of intriguing information about snakes of all kinds!

Learn all about these amazing creatures – the different kinds of snakes, where they live, the largest, the smallest, the most venomous, and more!

Unveil the mysteries of these mesmerizing creatures as we embark on a journey through their diverse habitats, behaviors, and adaptations.

So, what are you waiting for? Let's dive into the incredible and fascinating realm of snakes!

Enjoy!

MENTAL BOMB

Our goal is to entertain and to blow your mind!

Visit us online at MentalBomb.com
Home for the best illusions, riddles, games, and fun facts!

Follow

Facebook: Mental-Bomb-
Instagram: mental_bomb_
Pinterest: Mental_Bomb
Twitter: MentalBomb_

CONTENTS

1. What Are Snakes?

Snakes are fascinating reptiles known for their elongated bodies, lack of limbs, and unique adaptations that allow them to thrive in diverse environments across the world. These limbless creatures belong to the suborder Serpentes and are characterized by their ability to move through a variety of terrains using a method known as "serpentine locomotion," which involves bending and straightening their bodies in a wavelike motion.

One of the most distinctive features of snakes is their diverse range of sizes, colors, and patterns. From the vibrant and venomous coral snakes to the massive and powerful pythons, the variety in snake species is remarkable. Some snakes, like the anaconda and python, are known for their ability to constrict their prey, while others, like the black mamba and king cobra, have developed potent venom for hunting and defense.

Snakes play important ecological roles in various ecosystems. As predators, they help control populations of rodents and other small animals, contributing to the balance of nature. They are found in a wide range of habitats, including deserts, rainforests, grasslands, and aquatic environments. Some, like tree-dwelling boas and pythons, spend their lives in the trees, while others, like burrowing sand snakes, are adapted to life in arid landscapes.

While some snake species are venomous and pose risks to humans, the majority are harmless and often misunderstood. Snakes use a variety of defensive mechanisms, such as hissing, puffing up, or displaying vibrant colors, to deter predators or threats. Despite their sometimes fearsome reputation, snakes are an integral part of the natural world, contributing to biodiversity and offering a window into the fascinating adaptations that have allowed them to thrive over millions of years of evolution.

Research into snake biology, behavior, and ecology continues to unveil new insights about these intriguing creatures, shedding light on their interactions with other species and their roles in maintaining the delicate balance of ecosystems. Whether admired for their beauty, feared for their venom, or studied for their contributions to science, snakes remain a captivating subject of study and appreciation in the world of biology.

The following are 10 defining characteristics and critical facts about snakes:

1. **Body Structure:** Snakes have long, cylindrical bodies with a distinct head and tail. Their bodies are covered in scales, which help reduce water loss and provide protection.

2. **Limbless:** One of the defining features of snakes is their lack of limbs. They have evolved from reptiles with legs, and this limb reduction has allowed them to adapt to various habitats and ways of life.

3. **Habitats:** Snakes can be found in a range of habitats, including forests, deserts, grasslands, wetlands, and aquatic environments. They have adapted to both terrestrial and aquatic lifestyles.

4. **Feeding:** Snakes are carnivorous, which means they eat other animals. Their diet varies based on the species and size but can include rodents, birds, insects, and other reptiles.

5. **Hunting:** Many snakes are skilled predators. They use various methods to capture their prey, such as striking and constricting. Venomous snakes inject venom into their prey to immobilize or kill it.

6. **Reproduction:** Snakes reproduce either by laying eggs or giving birth to live young, depending on the species. Some snake species care for their eggs and protect them until they hatch.

7. **Venom:** Some snakes possess venom that they use for hunting or defense. Venomous snakes have specialized fangs and venom glands to deliver venom to their prey.

8. **Senses:** Snakes have well-developed senses, including excellent smell and the ability to sense vibrations through the ground. Some species also have heat-sensitive pits that help them locate warm-blooded prey.

9. **Biodiversity:** There are over 3,000 species of snakes, with a wide range of sizes and behaviors. They can be found on every continent except Antarctica.

10. **Conservation:** Like many other species, some snake populations are threatened due to habitat loss, pollution, and persecution. However, snakes also play important ecological roles, such as controlling rodent populations.

2. Snake Evolution

The evolution of snakes is a complex and fascinating journey that spans millions of years. Snakes are believed to have descended from ancient lizard-like ancestors, with their transition from limbed to limbless forms occurring over an extended period. The fossil record, comparative anatomy, and genetic evidence provide valuable insights into the evolutionary history of snakes.

The ancestors of modern snakes are thought to have lived during the Cretaceous period, around 100-150 million years ago. These early reptiles likely shared characteristics with modern lizards, but they began to adapt to different ecological niches, which led to changes in their body structure and behavior. One of the key adaptations that distinguish snakes from their ancestors is the reduction and eventual loss of limbs. Fossils of ancient snakes with vestigial hind limbs suggest a gradual reduction in limb size over generations.

One hypothesis regarding limb loss in snakes is related to their shift to burrowing lifestyles. Snakes that lived in underground environments may have benefited from having a more streamlined body without limbs, allowing them to move more efficiently through narrow tunnels and spaces. Over time, these limb-reduced forms had a survival advantage, and natural selection favored individuals with traits that enhanced their burrowing abilities.

Another significant adaptation in snake evolution is the development of specialized jaws and cranial features. Early snakes likely possessed mobile jaws that allowed them to consume larger prey compared to their lizard ancestors. This shift in feeding behavior might have been linked to the loss of limbs, as the ability to immobilize and consume prey without limbs became crucial. The evolution of venom delivery systems in some snake lineages further supported their transition to a carnivorous diet.

As snakes adapted to various habitats and ecological niches, they diversified into a wide array of species with varying body sizes, shapes, behaviors, and adaptations. This diversification led to the emergence of arboreal, aquatic, and terrestrial species, each suited to their specific environments and hunting strategies. The evolutionary story of snakes is a testament to the remarkable ways in which life forms adapt and specialize in response to their surroundings, resulting in the rich biodiversity of snake species we see today.

The following are 10 amazing facts about snake evolution:

1. **Limbs to Limbless:** Snakes evolved from ancient lizard ancestors, gradually losing their limbs over millions of years as they adapted to different habitats and lifestyles. Fossils of early snake relatives show tiny vestigial limbs, highlighting this transition.

2. **Hind Limbs:** Some modern snake species, like boas and pythons, still have tiny, claw-like remnants of hind limbs buried within their bodies. These remnants are evidence of their evolutionary history.

3. **Bizarre Skulls:** Snakes have unique skulls with numerous adaptations for swallowing large prey. Their jaws are highly flexible, allowing them to consume prey much larger than their heads by "walking" their jaws over the prey.

4. **Venom Evolution:** Venomous snakes evolved from non-venomous ancestors. Their venomous adaptations, including specialized fangs and venom glands, developed as tools for hunting, defense, and competition.

5. **Burrowing Innovations:** Some ancient snakes evolved to live in burrows and underground environments. These adaptations, including elongated bodies and reduced eyes, allowed them to thrive

in subterranean habitats.

6. **Early Sea Serpents:** Some of the earliest snake relatives were aquatic. Marine forms like the "mosasaurs" were large marine reptiles that occupied a niche like that of modern marine mammals.

7. **Adaptive Radiation:** Snakes underwent a rapid period of diversification during the Paleocene, leading to a wide variety of species adapted to different environments, prey types, and lifestyles.

8. **Vestigial Pelvic Spurs:** Many snake species possess tiny pelvic spurs, which are remnants of ancestral hind limbs. These spurs have sensory functions and are used during mating behavior in some species.

9. **Gliding Snakes:** A few snake species, such as the paradise tree snake, are capable of gliding through the air from tree to tree. They use their bodies to create a kind of "wing" and control their descent.

10. **Geographical Spread:** Snakes have dispersed across the globe, adapting to a remarkable range of environments. They are found on every continent except Antarctica, showcasing their evolutionary success.

3. Snake Diversity

Snakes are an incredibility diverse group with thousands of different snake species, each with its own unique characteristics, behaviors, and adaptations. Snakes can be categorized into various groups based on factors such as habitat, behavior, and physical features. Here are some common categories of snakes:

1. **Colubrids:** This is the largest family of snakes, encompassing a wide variety of species. Colubrids can be found in various habitats and exhibit diverse behaviors. Examples include garter snakes, rat snakes, and king snakes.

2. **Pythons:** These are large, non-venomous snakes known for their constricting abilities. Species like the reticulated python and ball python are popular in the pet trade.

3. **Boas:** Like pythons, boas are also non-venomous and include species like the boa constrictor. They are found in tropical regions and often have distinctive patterns.

4. **Vipers:** Vipers are a family of venomous snakes known for their triangular-shaped heads, heat-sensing pits, and retractable fangs. Examples include the rattlesnake and gaboon viper.

5. **Elapids:** Elapids are another family of venomous snakes, known for their potent neurotoxic venom. Species like the cobra, mamba, and coral snake are elapids.

6. **Sea Snakes:** These are venomous snakes that have adapted to marine environments. They possess flattened tails for swimming and can be found in the waters of the Pacific and Indian Oceans.

7. **Blind Snakes:** These small, burrowing snakes are often mistaken for worms due to their slender bodies and reduced eyesight. They are found in various parts of the world.

8. **File Snakes:** Also known as a hognose or shovel-nosed snake, these unique snakes have an upturned snout and are known for their dramatic defensive behaviors.

9. **Tree Snakes:** Arboreal snakes are adapted for life in trees. They often have prehensile tails and are capable of gliding through the air to move between trees.

10. **Sand Snakes:** These snakes are adapted to desert environments and have features such as pale coloration and specialized scales that help them move on loose sand.

These are just a few examples of the different kinds of snakes. In total, there are over 3,000 recognized species of snakes in the world. Snakes exhibit incredible diversity in terms of their appearance, behavior, and habitat preferences, making them a captivating subject of study for biologists and a source of wonder for nature enthusiasts.

4. Snake Biology

Snake biology encompasses the various aspects of the anatomy, physiology, behavior, and life history of snakes. Snakes are a diverse group of reptiles that have evolved a wide range of adaptations to suit their different habitats, diets, and survival strategies. Here's an overview of some key aspects of snake biology:

1. **Anatomy and Morphology:**
   - Snakes lack limbs, but some species retain tiny, vestigial structures where limbs would have been located in their evolutionary ancestors.
   - The body is elongated and cylindrical, divided into distinct sections: head, trunk, and tail.
   - The head is often wider than the body and contains specialized structures such as the skull, brain, eyes, and sensory organs.
   - Snakes have internal and external scales that provide protection, reduce water loss, and aid in movement.
   - Some species have specialized adaptations, such as heat-sensing pits (found in pit vipers) and specialized tails (prehensile tails in tree-dwelling species).

2. **Reproductive Biology:**
   - Snakes reproduce through sexual reproduction, with separate male and female individuals.
   - Some species lay eggs, while others give birth to live young. The method of reproduction depends on the species.

- Some snake species provide parental care to their eggs or young, guarding them and ensuring their survival.

3. **Feeding and Digestion:**
   - Snakes are carnivorous, meaning they primarily eat other animals.
   - Most snakes consume prey whole, using their flexible jaws to accommodate prey larger than their heads.
   - They have highly specialized digestive systems that can break down and absorb nutrients from the prey. Digestive enzymes and strong acids aid in this process.

4. **Venom and Defense:**
   - Many snake species have evolved venom as a means of subduing prey and defending against predators.
   - Venomous snakes have specialized venom glands and fangs for delivering venom to their prey or threats.
   - The composition and effects of snake venom can vary widely between species, ranging from neurotoxic to hemotoxic components.

5. **Behavior and Locomotion:**
   - Snakes exhibit diverse behaviors based on their habitats and lifestyles. Some are active during the day (diurnal), while others are active at night (nocturnal).
   - Locomotion methods include serpentine motion (slithering), sidewinding (adapted for sandy environments), and concertina movement (used for tight spaces and climbing).

6. **Ecosystem Roles:**
   - Snakes play crucial roles in ecosystems as both predators and prey. They help control populations of rodents and other small animals, contributing to ecosystem balance.
   - They also serve as a food source for larger predators, such as birds of prey and mammals.

7. **Sensory Perception:**
   - Snakes have a well-developed sense of smell, which they use to detect prey and navigate their environment.
   - Many snake species have specialized vision adapted to low light conditions, as well as heat-sensitive pits for detecting warm-blooded prey.

Understanding snake biology helps scientists and researchers gain insights into the evolutionary history, ecological roles, and adaptations of these intriguing and often misunderstood creatures.

5. Where Snakes Live – Habitats

Snakes are incredibly adaptable creatures that can be found in a wide range of habitats around the world. Their distribution spans diverse ecosystems, from tropical rainforests to deserts, grasslands, wetlands, mountains, and even aquatic environments. Here are some common habitats where snakes can be found:

1. **Forests:** Snakes inhabit various types of forests, including tropical rainforests, temperate forests, and deciduous forests. They can be found on the forest floor, in trees, and even in the leaf litter.

2. **Grasslands:** Snakes are often found in grasslands and savannas, where they can move through the vegetation in search of prey or shelter.

3. **Deserts:** Desert-dwelling snakes have adapted to arid conditions. They may burrow beneath the sand to escape extreme temperatures and find prey.

4. **Wetlands:** Snakes inhabit wetland areas such as marshes, swamps, and mangroves. They might be found near water sources, where they can find prey and stay hydrated.

5. **Mountains:** Some snake species can be found at high elevations in mountainous regions. These snakes have adapted to cooler temperatures and can be found in rocky crevices and alpine

meadows.

6. **Aquatic Environments:** Various snake species have adapted to aquatic habitats, including freshwater lakes, rivers, and even the open ocean. Sea snakes, for example, are fully adapted to marine life.

7. **Urban Areas:** Certain snake species have adapted to urban environments, where they can find shelter and food sources. Urban snakes might be found in gardens, parks, and even buildings.

8. **Burrows and Caves:** Burrowing snakes live underground, often in sandy or loose soil. Some species also inhabit caves and rocky crevices.

9. **Tundra:** Snakes in tundra environments have adapted to extremely cold conditions. They are typically smaller in size and can be found in areas with permafrost.

10. **Tropical Islands:** Many islands around the world are home to unique snake species that have evolved in isolation from mainland populations.

Snakes have evolved a wide range of adaptations that allow them to thrive in their specific habitats. These adaptations include coloration for camouflage, behaviors for hunting, and physiological traits for coping with temperature fluctuations and other environmental challenges. The diversity of snake habitats reflects their versatility and success as a group of reptiles that have colonized various niches across the planet.

6. Where Snakes Live – Continents

Snakes are found on every continent except Antarctica. They have adapted to a wide variety of ecosystems and habitats across the globe. Here's a breakdown of snake distribution by continent:

1. **North America:** Snakes inhabit North America, from the deserts of the southwestern United States to the forests of Canada. Some well-known species include:

   - **Garter Snake:** Garter snakes are widespread and can be found in various habitats. They are known for their distinct coloration and often have stripes running along their bodies.

   - **Eastern Rat Snake:** Also known as the black rat snake, this species is found in the eastern United States. It is non-venomous and can grow to a considerable length.

   - **Northern Water Snake:** These snakes inhabit aquatic environments and are often found near freshwater sources. They have dark bands on their bodies and are non-venomous.

   - **Western Rattlesnake:** Various species of rattlesnakes inhabit North America, known for their distinctive rattles on the tail. They are venomous and have a broad range across different regions.

- **Copperhead:** Found in the eastern and central United States, the copperhead is a venomous snake with a distinct pattern of bands and coloration.

- **Bullsnake:** Bullsnakes are non-venomous and are found in grasslands and open areas. They are known for their powerful hissing and defensive behaviors.

- **Northern Brown Snake:** These small snakes are found in a variety of habitats, from woodlands to gardens. They are non-venomous and have a distinctive pattern.

- **Ringneck Snake:** These small snakes have a unique ring or collar on their neck. They are found in various regions and are known for their vibrant belly colors.

- **Eastern Hognose Snake:** Hognose snakes are known for their dramatic defensive behaviors, including puffing up and playing dead. They are found in the eastern United States.

- **Corn Snake:** Corn snakes are popular in the pet trade and are found in southeastern and central United States. They are non-venomous and have distinctive patterns.

2. **South America:** The diverse rainforests, grasslands, and mountains of South America are home to a wide range of snake species, including anacondas, boas, and coral snakes. Some well-known species include:

- **Anaconda:** The green anaconda, one of the largest snakes in the world, is found in the Amazon rainforest and other aquatic habitats.

- **Boa Constrictor:** This non-venomous snake is found throughout South America and is known for its powerful constriction abilities.

- **Bushmaster:** These large venomous snakes are found in the rainforests of South America and are known for their potent venom.

- **Fer-de-Lance:** This genus of venomous pit vipers is found throughout Central and South America, including the Amazon rainforest.

- **Coral Snake:** Coral snakes are venomous and have striking color patterns. They are found in various regions across South America.

- **Rainbow Boa:** This non-venomous snake is known for its iridescent scales and is found in tropical rainforests.

- **South American Rattlesnake:** These venomous snakes are found in different habitats, including grasslands and rainforests.

- **South American False Coral Snake:** These non-venomous snakes mimic the appearance of coral snakes but lack their potent venom.

- **Yellow Anaconda:** Smaller than the green anaconda, the yellow anaconda is found in wetlands and aquatic habitats.

- **Amazon Tree Boa:** This non-venomous snake is arboreal and found in the canopy of rainforests.

3. **Europe:** Snakes are found in parts of Europe, including the Mediterranean region. Some well-known species include:

- **European Adder:** Also known as the common adder, this venomous snake is found in various habitats across Europe, including grasslands and woodlands.

- **Smooth Snake:** Non-venomous and often mistaken for vipers, the smooth snake is found in parts of Western Europe.

- **Grass Snake:** Non-venomous and aquatic, grass snakes are found in wetlands and near water sources in Europe.

- **Aesculapian Snake:** Non-venomous and tree-dwelling, these snakes are found in parts of southern and central Europe.

- **Dice Snake:** Non-venomous and aquatic, the dice snake inhabits freshwater habitats and can be found in various regions.

- **Viperine Snake:** This non-venomous snake is often found near water sources and has a diet that includes amphibians and fish.

- **Smooth-headed Snake:** Non-venomous and found in parts of Southern Europe, these snakes are known for their distinctive head shape.

- **Montpellier Snake:** Non-venomous and diurnal, this snake is found in Mediterranean regions and grasslands.

- **European Cat Snake:** Non-venomous and often found in

rocky habitats, these snakes have a unique appearance.

- **Horseshoe Whip Snake:** Non-venomous and found in southern Europe, these snakes are known for their slender bodies.

4. **Asia:** Asia is home to a rich diversity of snake species due to its varied landscapes. Snakes such as the Indian python, king cobra, and various vipers inhabit this continent. Some well-known species include:

   - **Indian Cobra:** This venomous snake is found in a wide range of habitats across the Indian subcontinent and is known for its distinctive hood.

   - **Russell's Viper:** Another venomous snake in Asia, the Russell's viper is found in grasslands and forests and is known for its potent venom.

   - **King Cobra:** The largest venomous snake in the world, the king cobra is found in Southeast Asia and is known for its ability to eat other snakes.

   - **Common Krait:** This venomous snake is often found near human settlements and is known for its nocturnal habits.

   - **Rat Snake:** Rat snakes are non-venomous and found in various habitats across Asia. They are known for their adaptability.

   - **Banded Krait:** Another venomous krait species, the banded krait is found in Southeast Asia and is recognized by its striking black and white bands.

- **Copperhead Racer:** This non-venomous snake is often found in agricultural areas and can climb trees.

- **Chinese Rat Snake**: Non-venomous and found in China, this snake is known for its distinct coloration and pattern.

- **Indian Rock Python:** One of the largest snake species, the Indian rock python is found in a variety of habitats across the Indian subcontinent.

- **Taiwan Beauty Snake:** Non-venomous and found in Taiwan, this snake is known for its attractive coloration.

5. **Africa:** The continent of Africa hosts a wide array of snake species, from the deserts of the Sahara to the lush rainforests. African snakes include puff adders, mambas, and boomslangs. Some well-known species include:

- **Puff Adder:** This venomous snake is known for its cryptic coloration and is found in a wide range of habitats across Africa.

- **Black Mamba**: One of the fastest and most venomous snakes in the world, the black mamba is found in various regions of sub-Saharan Africa.

- **Cape Cobra:** This venomous cobra species is found in southern Africa and is known for its hood and variable coloration.

- **Boomslang**: This arboreal snake is found in sub-Saharan Africa and is known for its potent venom.

- **African Rock Python**: One of the largest snake species, the African rock python is found in a variety of habitats across sub-Saharan Africa.

- **Gaboon Viper**: This venomous snake is known for its large, triangular head and is found in rainforests and woodlands.

- **Egyptian Cobra**: This venomous cobra species is found in various regions across Africa, including the Sahara Desert.

- **Puff-faced Water Snake:** Non-venomous and aquatic, this snake is found in freshwater habitats across sub-Saharan Africa.

- **Twig Snake:** These slender snakes are found in various regions and are known for their cryptic coloration and habits.

- **African Egg-Eating Snake**: Non-venomous and found in sub-Saharan Africa, these snakes have specialized diets of eggs.

6. **Australia:** Snakes in Australia have evolved in isolation, leading to a unique assemblage of species. The continent is home to various venomous snakes like the taipan and brown snake, as well as non-venomous species like the carpet python. Some well-known species include:

   - **Eastern Brown Snake:** This venomous snake is highly variable in color and is found in a wide range of habitats across eastern and southeastern Australia.

- **Red-bellied Black Snake:** This non-venomous snake is known for its striking red belly and is found in various habitats, including wetlands and forests.

- **Coastal Taipan:** This venomous snake is found in coastal areas of northern and eastern Australia and is known for its potent venom.

- **Common Tree Snake:** Non-venomous and arboreal, this snake is found in a variety of habitats, including rainforests and urban areas.

- **Inland Taipan:** Also known as the "fierce snake," this is one of the most venomous snakes in the world. It is found in central Australia.

- **Mulga Snake:** This venomous snake is found in arid and semi-arid regions of Australia and is known for its distinctive black and white bands.

- **King Brown Snake:.** It is highly venomous and found in a variety of habitats across Australia.

- **Spotted Python:** Non-venomous and often kept as a pet, this snake is found in northern and eastern Australia.

- **Children's Python:** Non-venomous and relatively small, this python species is found in northern and eastern Australia.

- **Stimson's Python:** Non-venomous and found in northern and central Australia, this python is known for its docile nature.

7. Where Snakes Live – Water

Aquatic snakes are snake species that have adapted to living primarily in aquatic environments, such as rivers, lakes, swamps, and oceans. These snakes have evolved specific traits and behaviors that enable them to thrive in water.

Here are some characteristics commonly associated with aquatic snakes:

1. **Body Shape:** Aquatic snakes usually have a streamlined body shape that helps them move through water with minimal resistance. This adaptation is like that of eels and other aquatic animals.

2. **Scale Arrangement:** Many aquatic snake species have scales that are keeled, which means they have a ridge running down the center. This helps provide better grip in aquatic environments and assists with swimming.

3. **Valves in Nostrils:** Some aquatic snakes possess valves or flaps in their nostrils that allow them to close their nostrils while submerged. This prevents water from entering their respiratory system.

4. **Specialized Respiratory Adaptations:** Aquatic snakes can hold their breath for extended periods of time. They have adapted respiratory systems that allow them to extract oxygen from both water and air, making them well-suited to life in aquatic habitats.

5. **Strong Swimmers:** Aquatic snakes are skilled swimmers. They use lateral undulation, similar to the way other snakes move on land, but with more emphasis on pushing against the water to propel

themselves forward.

6. **Prey Adaptations:** Aquatic snakes often feed on aquatic animals, such as fish, amphibians, and crustaceans. They have specialized adaptations for capturing and consuming their aquatic prey.

7. **Habitat Preferences:** Depending on the species, aquatic snakes can be found in freshwater or saltwater habitats. Some live in rivers, lakes, and swamps, while others are adapted to marine environments and can be found in coastal waters and oceans.

8. **Venomous vs. Non-venomous:** There are both venomous and non-venomous aquatic snake species. Venomous aquatic snakes use their venom to immobilize or kill prey and, in some cases, for defense.

There are numerous species of aquatic snakes found around the world, each adapted to different aquatic environments and habitats. There are well over 100 recognized species of sea snakes alone. Additionally, many non-venomous snakes also have adaptations for living in aquatic environments. Some of the most well-known aquatic and semi-aquatic snakes include the following:

1. **Green Anaconda:** The green anaconda is one of the largest snake species in the world and is well-adapted to life in aquatic environments. It's found in South America and is known for its ability to thrive in swamps, marshes, and slow-moving rivers.

2. **Common Water Snake:** Found in North America, the common water snake is a non-venomous species that inhabits various aquatic habitats such as lakes, ponds, and slow-moving streams.

3. **Olive Sea Snake:** This sea snake is found in the Indo-Pacific region and is known for its striking olive-green coloration. It's a highly venomous species that primarily lives in coral reefs and

shallow coastal waters.

4. **Cottonmouth:** Also known as the water moccasin, the cottonmouth is a venomous snake found in the southeastern United States. It's often associated with aquatic environments like swamps, marshes, and slow-moving waters.

5. **Yellow-Bellied Sea Snake:** This sea snake is known for its distinctive bright yellow underside. It's found in tropical and subtropical oceans and is one of the most widely distributed sea snake species.

6. **Banded Sea Krait:** This sea krait is found in the Pacific and Indian Oceans. It has distinctive bands of color on its body and is known for its unique hunting behavior, which involves entering water to feed on eels and fish.

7. **Estuarine Sea Snake:** Another member of the sea krait group, this species is found in coastal waters and estuaries in the Indo-Pacific region. It has a more subdued coloration compared to other sea kraits.

8. **Red-Bellied Black Snake:** Found in Australia, this snake is known for its black body and red or orange belly. It inhabits a variety of habitats, including wetlands and waterways.

9. **Keel-Bellied Water Snake:** Found in parts of Asia, this non-venomous snake lives in a range of aquatic environments, including ponds, rivers, and rice paddies.

10. **Rainbow Water Snake:** This snake is found in Southeast Asia and is known for its vibrant coloration. It's typically found near water bodies and feeds on aquatic prey.

Additionally, aquatic and semi-aquatic snakes have some fascinating adaptations and behaviors that set them apart. Here are 10 amazing facts about these some of these snakes and the adaptations they have to help them thrive in aquatic or semi-aquatic environments:

1. **Dual Respiration:** Aquatic snakes have developed the ability to respire through their skin and mouth while underwater. This allows them to extract oxygen from both water and air, enabling prolonged dives.

2. **Valves in Nostrils:** Many aquatic snakes possess specialized valves in their nostrils that allow them to close them when submerged. This prevents water from entering their respiratory system.

3. **Salt Excretion:** Sea snakes have specialized glands near their tongues that help excrete excess salt from their bodies, enabling them to live in saltwater environments.

4. **Pelagic Lifestyle:** Some sea snakes never come to shore, spending their entire lives in the open ocean. They give birth to live young at sea, reducing the need to return to land.

5. **Viviparity:** Many aquatic snakes, including sea snakes, give birth to live offspring instead of laying eggs. This adaptation ensures the survival of their young in aquatic environments.

6. **Venom Adaptations:** Venomous aquatic snakes, like sea snakes, often have short fangs positioned at the front of their mouths, allowing them to bite and inject venom into fish and other prey more efficiently.

7. **Strong Swimmers:** Aquatic snakes use a specialized form of movement called lateral undulation to swim efficiently. This involves bending their bodies from side to side to push against the

water.

8. **Camouflage and Mimicry:** Some aquatic snakes, like the banded sea krait, have coloration that mimics the appearance of coral reefs, helping them blend in and avoid predators.

9. **Marine Migration:** Sea snakes undertake impressive migrations, traveling long distances between their breeding and feeding grounds. Some species have been recorded traveling thousands of kilometers.

10. **Unique Hunting Techniques:** Some aquatic snakes employ clever hunting strategies. For example, the rainbow water snake uses its bright colors to attract fish, luring them within striking range.

These adaptations and behaviors illustrate the remarkable ways in which aquatic snakes have evolved to thrive in their watery habitats.

8. The Largest Snakes

Some snakes can grow to enormous sizes. For example, the largest anaconda was reportedly 33 feet long, 3 feet across at its widest part, and weighed about 880 lbs. This snake was discovered at a construction site in Brazil. Additionally, the largest python ever recorded was a reticulated python found in 1912 in Indonesia that was 33 feet long.

In addition to those two behemoths, the following are the largest snake species in the world:

1. **Green Anaconda (Eunectes murinus)**: The green anaconda is considered the largest snake in the world in terms of sheer mass. It can reach lengths of up to 25 feet or more and weigh over 500 pounds. These massive snakes are found in the rainforests of South America, particularly in the Amazon basin. They are powerful constrictors, using their massive bodies to suffocate and overpower their prey, which includes a variety of mammals, birds, and aquatic creatures.

2. **Reticulated Python (Python reticulatus)**: The reticulated python is known for being one of the longest snake species. It can grow up to about 23 feet in length, although some individuals have been reported to exceed this size. These pythons are found in Southeast Asia and are known for their intricate pattern of scales. They are ambush predators that mainly feed on mammals and birds, using their powerful bodies to wrap around and constrict their prey.

3. **African Rock Python (Python sebae)**: African rock pythons can reach lengths of around 20 feet. They inhabit a wide range of environments across sub-Saharan Africa, including grasslands, savannas, and forests. These pythons are non-venomous and use constriction to capture and kill their prey, which can include mammals as large as antelope and crocodiles.

4. **Burmese Python (Python bivittatus)**: Native to Southeast Asia, Burmese pythons can grow up to around 18 feet in length. They have become invasive in certain areas outside their native range, such as in Florida, USA. These pythons are excellent swimmers and climbers, and they are known for their striking pattern of dark blotches on a light background.

5. **Indian Python (Python molurus)**: The Indian python, also known as the Indian rock python, can reach lengths of up to 18 feet. They are found in a variety of habitats across the Indian subcontinent and Southeast Asia. Like other large pythons, they rely on constriction to subdue their prey, which includes mammals and birds.

6. **Amethystine Python (Morelia amethystina)**: The amethystine python, also known as the scrub python, is native to northern Australia, New Guinea, and nearby islands. It can reach lengths of up to 16 feet. These pythons are often found in forests and dense vegetation, and they are known for their iridescent sheen.

9.   The Smallest Snakes

While some snakes can grow to enormous sizes, some are incredibly small.   The world's smallest snake species belong to the families Leptotyphlopidae and Typhlopidae. These snakes are commonly referred to as threadsnakes or blind snakes due to their tiny size and often fossorial (burrowing) habits. Here are a few examples of some of the smallest snake species:

1. **Barbados Threadsnake (Tetracheilostoma carlae)**: Native to the Caribbean island of Barbados, this species holds the title for the smallest snake in the world. Adults typically reach lengths of about 4 inches (10 centimeters) or even less.

2. **Leptotyphlops carlae**: This snake, often referred to as Carla's threadsnake, is also among the smallest snakes. It's closely related to the Barbados threadsnake and is similarly tiny, with adults measuring only a few inches in length.

3. **Western Blind Snake (Leptotyphlops humilis)**: Found in the southwestern United States and northern Mexico, this species is extremely small, usually measuring around 4 to 6 inches (10 to 15 centimeters) in length.

4. **Kitti's Hog-nosed Snake (Leptotyphlops kitti)**: Formerly known as the "world's smallest snake," Kitti's hog-nosed snake is native to Southeast Asia. Adults typically reach lengths of about 4.1 to 4.3 inches (10.4 to 10.9 centimeters).

5. **Texas Blind Snake (Leptotyphlops dulcis)**: This species is found in the southern United States and parts of Mexico. It's a small snake, usually measuring around 6 to 7 inches (15 to 18 centimeters) in length.

6. **Indotyphlops braminus**: Commonly known as the Brahminy blind snake, this species is found in many parts of the world, often in association with human habitation. It's small, usually measuring around 6 to 8 inches (15 to 20 centimeters) in length.

These tiny snakes have evolved to thrive in their underground habitats and are adapted for a burrowing lifestyle. They often feed on ants and other small insects.

10. The Most Venomous Snakes

Ranking the most venomous snakes is a complex task, as venom toxicity can be assessed using various factors, including LD50 (lethal dose for 50% of test subjects), the potency of specific venom components, and the effects of envenomation on humans.

Additionally, venom potency can vary between individual snakes within a species and even among different populations of the same species. With that in mind, here's a rough ranking of some of the most venomous snakes, based on their reputation for potent venom and their potential to cause harm to humans:

1. **Inland Taipan:** Often considered the most venomous snake, the inland taipan's venom has extremely potent neurotoxic components. However, it's important to note that human encounters with this snake are very rare.

2. **Belcher's Sea Snake::** Found in the Indian and Pacific Oceans, this snake produces highly toxic venom, containing potent neurotoxins.

3. **Coastal Taipan:** Native to Australia, the coastal taipan has venom with potent neurotoxic components, making it highly dangerous.

4. **Black Mamba:** The black mamba's venom is rich in neurotoxins and has a rapid onset of symptoms. Its speed and aggression contribute to its reputation as a deadly snake.

5. **King Cobra**: This large snake has a combination of potent neurotoxic and cytotoxic venom, making it extremely dangerous.

6. **Many-Banded Krait**: The venom of the many-banded krait is highly neurotoxic and can cause paralysis, making it a serious threat to humans.

7. **Russell's Viper**: With hemotoxic venom that can lead to tissue damage and coagulopathy, the Russell's viper is responsible for many snakebite fatalities.

8. **Saw-Scaled Viper**: Saw-scaled vipers have hemotoxic venom and are known for their aggressive behavior, which can lead to bites.

9. **Death Adder**: Death adders possess neurotoxic venom that can induce paralysis, and they are skilled ambush predators.

10. **Many-Banded Sea Snake**: Another highly venomous sea snake, the many-banded sea snake is known for its potent neurotoxic venom.

11. Anacondas

Anacondas are a group of large, non-venomous snakes primarily found in the lush rainforests and waterways of South America. The term "anaconda" commonly refers to the green anaconda (Eunectes murinus), which is the largest snake species in terms of weight. These impressive serpents can grow to lengths exceeding 25 feet and weigh over 500 pounds. Known for their semi-aquatic nature, anacondas are excellent swimmers, using their muscular bodies to navigate waterways in search of prey, which can include mammals, birds, and aquatic creatures.

Anacondas are revered for their powerful constriction abilities, which they use to subdue and suffocate their prey. Despite their massive size, they possess a certain level of adaptability, allowing them to inhabit a range of environments, from dense rainforests to swamps and rivers. Green anacondas, in particular, have an intricate pattern of dark greenish-black spots on their back that helps them blend into their surroundings, making them effective ambush predators.

The mystique surrounding anacondas, their massive size, and their role as apex predators within their ecosystems have made them a subject of fascination and curiosity for both scientists and the public. While they are known for their potential to capture large prey and their significant place in South American folklore, encounters with these majestic creatures in the wild are relatively rare due to their elusive behavior.

Fun Facts about Anacondas:

1. **Size and Strength**: Anacondas are famous for their immense size and strength. They are among the largest snakes globally and possess

powerful constricting abilities that allow them to overpower and suffocate their prey.

2. **Eating Habits**: These snakes are known to swallow their prey whole after constricting it. They have incredibly flexible jaws that allow them to consume animals much larger than their heads.

3. **Aquatic Lifestyle**: Anacondas are semi-aquatic, spending much of their time in or near water. They are excellent swimmers and can stay submerged for long periods, using their eyes and nostrils positioned on the tops of their heads to observe their surroundings while mostly hidden underwater.

4. **Lurking Predators**: They are ambush predators, patiently waiting in the water for animals to come close before striking with a rapid attack.

5. **Myths and Legends**: Anacondas have captured the imagination of people worldwide, often leading to myths and legends about their size and behavior. While some accounts may be exaggerated, these snakes are indeed impressive creatures with adaptations that make them successful predators in their ecosystems.

12. Black Mambas

The Black Mamba is one of the most feared and venomous snakes in the world, found predominantly in sub-Saharan Africa. Despite their name, they are typically olive to grayish-brown in color, with a light-colored belly. Renowned for their incredible speed, black mambas are among the fastest snakes, capable of reaching speeds of up to 12 mph (19 km/h) over short distances. Their agility makes them efficient hunters, capable of covering large areas in search of prey.

Equipped with potent neurotoxic venom, black mambas are considered one of the deadliest snakes in the world. The venom targets the nervous system, leading to rapid paralysis if not treated promptly with antivenom. These snakes are adaptable and can thrive in various habitats, including savannas, woodlands, and rocky terrain. Despite their venomous nature, black mambas are generally non-aggressive and prefer to escape rather than confront threats. However, they can become defensive if cornered or provoked, displaying their dark mouths as a warning signal to potential predators.

Black mambas play a vital ecological role by helping control rodent populations, which in turn affects the balance of their ecosystems. Their reputation as formidable and dangerous snakes contributes to the intrigue and fear that surrounds them, making them a subject of interest in the realm of herpetology and natural history.

Fun Facts about Black Mambas:

1. **Speed Demons**: Black mambas are known for their incredible speed, capable of covering large distances in a short amount of

time. Their agility makes them efficient hunters and difficult to evade.

2. **Tree Climbers**: While terrestrial, black mambas are excellent climbers. They can ascend trees with ease to escape predators or to hunt for birds and eggs.

3. **Venom Potency**: The venom of the black mamba is both highly toxic and fast-acting. A bite can lead to paralysis and death in a matter of hours if not treated promptly with antivenom.

4. **Distinctive Defense**: When threatened, black mambas raise their heads and a portion of their upper bodies off the ground, displaying their dark mouths as a warning signal to potential predators.

5. **Long, Slender Bodies**: Black mambas are characterized by their long, slender bodies that can reach lengths of up to 14 feet (4.3 meters). They have a relatively small head compared to their body size.

13. Boomslangs

The Boomslang (Dispholidus typus) is a venomous snake species native to sub-Saharan Africa. Its name originates from Afrikaans and Dutch words meaning "tree snake," which reflects its arboreal lifestyle. Boomslangs are known for their distinct sexual dimorphism in coloration. Males are vibrant green, while females are typically brown or green with lighter bellies. This coloration aids in their camouflage while hunting in trees.

Despite being venomous, the boomslang is not considered a direct threat to humans due to its non-aggressive nature and reclusive behavior. The snake's venom contains potent hemotoxins that interfere with blood clotting, potentially leading to internal bleeding. However, bites and envenomations are rare, mainly occurring when the snake feels cornered or threatened. The boomslang primarily preys on small vertebrates and eggs, and its rear-fanged delivery system allows it to incapacitate its prey through venom injected while chewing or gnawing.

The boomslang's role in its ecosystem is to control populations of birds and their eggs, making it an essential contributor to maintaining ecological balance. Despite its venomous attributes, the boomslang is a fascinating and somewhat enigmatic snake species, adding to the rich biodiversity of the African continent.

Fun Facts about Boomslang:

1. **Color Variation**: Boomslangs exhibit sexual dimorphism in color. Males are typically bright green, while females are a more subdued green or brown. This coloration helps them blend into their surroundings.

2. **Egg Eaters**: Boomslangs are known for their unique feeding habits. They primarily consume eggs and small vertebrates, and their jaw structure allows them to eat eggs without breaking them.

3. **Rear-Fanged Venomous**: Unlike front-fanged snakes that deliver venom through hollow fangs at the front of their mouth, boomslangs have rear-fangs that are positioned toward the back of their upper jaw. This allows them to deliver venom by chewing or gnawing on their prey.

4. **Arboreal Lifestyle**: Boomslangs are excellent climbers, spending much of their time in trees where they hunt for birds and their eggs. Their laterally compressed bodies help them maneuver through foliage.

5. **Venom and Bites**: While boomslangs have potent venom, their non-aggressive nature means they rarely pose a threat to humans. Bites are uncommon, however, if bitten, prompt medical attention is essential due to the potential for serious bleeding disorders caused by their venom.

14. Bush Vipers

The Bush Viper refers to a group of venomous snakes belonging to the genus Atheris. These striking serpents are known for their vibrant coloration and unique appearance. Found in parts of sub-Saharan Africa, bush vipers inhabit various forested habitats, including rainforests and montane forests. Their small size and remarkable ability to blend into their surroundings make them both intriguing and elusive creatures.

Bush vipers are characterized by their triangular-shaped heads and vertically oriented pupils, which are adaptations for their arboreal lifestyle. They often perch on branches or vegetation, waiting to ambush unsuspecting prey that wanders by. One of the most distinctive features of bush vipers is their color diversity, ranging from bright green and blue to yellow and even shades of red or orange. This coloration provides effective camouflage among the leaves and branches of their habitat, making them difficult to spot for both predators and potential prey.

While their appearance is captivating, bush vipers are venomous and possess potent hemotoxic venom that can lead to tissue damage and other harmful effects. Due to their relatively small size and reclusive nature, interactions between bush vipers and humans are rare, but their unique beauty and role in their ecosystems make them a subject of interest for herpetologists and enthusiasts alike.

Fun Facts about Bush Vipers:

1. **Vivid Coloration:** Bush vipers are known for their dazzling and varied coloration. They can come in shades of green, blue, yellow, red, and even orange. This colorful appearance helps them blend

into the foliage of their forested habitats, making them excellent ambush predators.

2. **Small Size**: Bush vipers are relatively small snakes, with lengths ranging from about 20 to 75 centimeters (8 to 30 inches), depending on the species. Despite their small size, their venom is potent and adapted for their hunting strategy.

3. **Vertical Pupils**: These vipers have vertical pupils, which are well-suited for their arboreal lifestyle. Vertical pupils help them control the amount of light that enters their eyes, allowing them to better focus on their prey and surroundings.

4. **Prehensile Tail**: Some species of bush vipers have prehensile tails, meaning their tails are adapted for grasping objects, such as branches. This helps them maintain their position while perched on vegetation.

5. **Viviparous Reproduction**: Unlike many other viper species, which lay eggs, most bush vipers give birth to live young. This reproductive strategy is known as viviparity. The female retains the developing embryos internally, providing them with protection and nourishment until they are ready to be born.

15. Coral Snakes

Coral Snakes are a group of venomous snakes belonging to the family Elapidae, found in various regions of North and South America. They are known for their striking coloration, which often consists of bright bands of red, yellow, and black. The "red on yellow, kill a fellow; red on black, venom lack" rhyme is a common mnemonic used to distinguish between venomous coral snakes and non-venomous look-alike species like scarlet king snakes.

Coral snakes have potent neurotoxic venom that affects the nervous system and can cause paralysis if not treated promptly. Despite their venomous nature, coral snakes are generally reclusive and have relatively small mouths, which makes biting larger animals, including humans, more difficult. They often rely on a chewing action to inject venom, which means that bites might not always result in envenomation.

Coral snakes are primarily ground-dwelling and are often found in forests, grasslands, and scrublands. They feed on small prey, such as other snakes, lizards, and amphibians. Due to their relatively secretive behavior and the difficulty of obtaining enough venom to deliver a dangerous bite, coral snake bites to humans are rare. However, if bitten, seeking medical attention promptly is crucial due to the potential severity of envenomation.

Fun Facts about Coral Snakes:

1. **Colorful Warning Signals**: Coral snakes are known for their distinctive coloration of red, yellow, and black bands. Their bright and contrasting colors serve as a warning to potential predators, signaling their venomous nature. The common rhyme "red on yellow, kill a fellow; red on black, venom lack" helps people differentiate between venomous coral snakes and harmless look-alike species.

2. **Elapid Relatives**: Coral snakes are part of the Elapidae family, which includes other venomous snakes like cobras and mambas. Their venom contains neurotoxins that affect the nervous system and can lead to paralysis.

3. **Rear-Fanged Venom Delivery**: Coral snakes have relatively small mouths and use a chewing motion to deliver venom. Unlike vipers, which have large fangs at the front of their mouths, coral snakes' fangs are positioned toward the back of their mouths.

4. **Reclusive Behavior**: Coral snakes are generally shy and reclusive, preferring to avoid confrontation. Their secretive nature contributes to their relatively low incidence of bites to humans.

5. **Mimicry and Misidentification**: Some non-venomous snakes, like scarlet king snakes, closely resemble coral snakes in terms of coloration. This mimicry is thought to offer protection by capitalizing on the predator avoidance learned from the distinctive colors of true coral snakes. However, this mimicry also leads to instances of misidentification, and the rhyme is a useful tool for distinguishing between the two.

16. Emerald Tree Boas

The Emerald Tree Boa (Corallus caninus) is a visually stunning and non-venomous snake species found in the rainforests of South America, particularly in countries like Brazil, Colombia, and Peru. This arboreal snake is known for its vibrant emerald green coloration, which provides excellent camouflage among the lush foliage of its habitat. Its coloration, combined with its coiled posture and distinctive head shape, makes it a remarkable sight in the treetops.

Emerald tree boas are equipped with prehensile tails that allow them to coil around branches securely, enhancing their ability to navigate through the trees. They are primarily nocturnal hunters, relying on their ambush skills to capture prey like birds, small mammals, and occasionally other small reptiles. Despite their formidable appearance, emerald tree boas are generally docile and slow-moving, which makes them a popular choice among reptile enthusiasts.

One of the most captivating features of the emerald tree boa is its striking pattern of white or pale-yellow markings that contrast beautifully with its vibrant green body. This species showcases the diverse adaptations and beauty found within the intricate ecosystems of the rainforests, where they play a role in controlling prey populations and maintaining the balance of the food web.

Fun Facts about Emerald Tree Boas:

1. **Striking Coloration:** The emerald tree boa is renowned for its vibrant emerald green color, which helps it blend seamlessly into the green foliage of its rainforest habitat. This camouflage allows it to remain concealed from both predators and prey.

2. **Unique Head Shape**: The snake's head has a distinctive shape, with a somewhat triangular appearance. This, combined with its coloration, contributes to its striking and recognizable look.

3. **Prehensile Tail**: Emerald tree boas possess a prehensile tail that acts like an extra hand, allowing them to secure themselves to branches and maneuver with ease in their arboreal environment.

4. **Coiled Ambush Predators**: These snakes are skilled ambush predators. They use their coiled posture to hide among the branches, waiting for unsuspecting prey like birds and small mammals to come within striking range.

5. **Non-Venomous Constrictors**: Despite their impressive appearance, emerald tree boas are non-venomous constrictor snakes. They use their powerful bodies to subdue and constrict their prey, making them skilled hunters of the treetops.

17. Gaboon Vipers

The Gaboon Viper (Bitis gabonica) is a highly venomous snake species found in the tropical rainforests and savannas of sub-Saharan Africa. Known for its unique and intricate pattern, the Gaboon viper boasts one of the most distinctive and remarkable appearances among snakes. It has a broad, triangular head with a prominent, horn-like projection above each eye. These projections, called "supraocular horns," add to its intriguing look and serve as a form of camouflage among leaf litter and forest floors.

Gaboon vipers are ambush predators, relying on their cryptic coloration to remain concealed while waiting for prey to pass by. Their venom is potent and hemotoxic, causing tissue damage, pain, and potentially serious medical complications if envenomation occurs. Despite their venomous nature, they are generally not aggressive and prefer to remain hidden rather than confront potential threats. However, when disturbed or threatened, they may strike in self-defense.

The Gaboon viper's distinctive appearance, potent venom, and secretive behavior make it both a subject of fascination and caution. Its role as a predator in its ecosystem contributes to the balance of prey populations and the overall health of the African habitats it inhabits.

Fun Facts about Gaboon Viper::

1. **Horned Appearance**: The Gaboon viper is known for its unique and unmistakable appearance, characterized by the large, horn-like projections above its eyes. These supraocular horns are more prominent in females and play a role in the snake's camouflage by breaking up its outline and resembling leaf litter.

2. **Camouflaged Expert**: Gaboon vipers have an intricate and cryptic pattern on their scales, resembling the dappled light and shadows of their forest and savanna habitats. This camouflage helps them blend into their surroundings, making them well-suited for ambush hunting.

3. **Long Fangs**: These vipers possess some of the longest fangs of any snake, measuring up to 2 inches (5 centimeters) in length. These fangs are used to inject their venom deep into their prey.

4. **Venom and Fangs**: The Gaboon viper's venom is highly potent and hemotoxic, causing tissue damage and coagulation issues in its prey. Despite its potency, the snake's slow-moving nature and preference for staying hidden mean that human encounters are relatively rare.

5. **Large Size**: Gaboon vipers are among the largest vipers in Africa, with some individuals reaching lengths of over 5 feet (1.5 meters). Their robust size contributes to their role as top predators in their ecosystems.

18. Garter Snakes

Garter snakes are a widespread group of non-venomous colubrid snakes found throughout North and Central America. They are known for their relatively small size, distinct coloration, and adaptability to various habitats, making them one of the most recognizable and frequently encountered snake species in the region. Garter snakes are often considered harmless and even beneficial to humans due to their role in controlling pest populations.

These snakes come in a range of color variations, with some species displaying vibrant patterns of stripes and spots along their bodies. One common characteristic is a longitudinal stripe down the back, often accompanied by smaller lateral stripes. Garter snakes are known for their keen swimming abilities and can often be found near water sources, where they hunt for prey such as fish, amphibians, and insects.

Garter snakes are notable for their behavior of giving birth to live young, a trait relatively uncommon among snake species. They are also known for their willingness to release a foul-smelling musk as a defensive tactic when threatened, which serves to deter predators. Their adaptability to different environments, varied diets, and relatively benign nature have made garter snakes a popular subject of study and observation for both herpetology enthusiasts and researchers.

Fun Facts about Garter Snakes:

1. **Live Birth**: Unlike many other snake species, garter snakes give birth to live young instead of laying eggs. This reproductive

strategy is called viviparity. Female garter snakes retain the developing embryos inside their bodies until they are ready to be born.

2. **Variety of Habitats**: Garter snakes are incredibly adaptable and can be found in a wide range of habitats, including grasslands, forests, wetlands, and even urban areas. Their ability to thrive in various environments contributes to their widespread distribution.

3. **Keen Swimmers**: Garter snakes are excellent swimmers and are often found near water sources, such as ponds, streams, and even backyard gardens with water features. They are skilled at catching aquatic prey like fish, tadpoles, and frogs.

4. **Musk Defense**: When threatened, garter snakes have a unique defensive behavior. They emit a foul-smelling musk from their cloacal glands, which is accompanied by a rapid vibration of the tail. This behavior helps deter predators and is often effective in keeping potential threats at bay.

5. **Heterogeneous Diet**: Garter snakes have a diverse diet that includes insects, small mammals, amphibians, fish, and even earthworms. Their varied palate makes them important contributors to ecosystem balance by helping control populations of pests and other small creatures.

19. Green Tree Pythons

The Green Tree Python (Morelia viridis) is a visually striking snake species known for its vibrant green coloration and its arboreal lifestyle. Found in the rainforests of New Guinea, Indonesia, and nearby regions, this snake spends much of its life in the trees, coiled around branches and vegetation. The green color helps it blend seamlessly into the lush canopy, making it a remarkable and elusive sight.

Green tree pythons have a unique method of hunting. They are ambush predators, using their exceptional camouflage to hide among leaves and branches, waiting for prey to approach. When a suitable meal comes into striking range, the snake will swiftly grasp the prey in its coiled body. Despite their vivid green appearance, they can also exhibit blue coloration, particularly in certain populations.

One of the captivating features of green tree pythons is their prehensile tail, which they use to anchor themselves securely to branches. This specialized adaptation allows them to rest, hunt, and move efficiently in the treetops. Their docile temperament and captivating appearance have made them popular among reptile enthusiasts, although their care requirements can be quite specific due to their arboreal nature and unique characteristics.

Fun Facts about Green Tree Pythons:

1. **Vivid Color Variations**: While their name suggests a green color, Green Tree Pythons can display a range of colors, including bright green, blue, and even yellow. These color variations are thought to

be influenced by factors such as lighting, temperature, and camouflage needs.

2. **Arboreal Lifestyle**: Green Tree Pythons are perfectly adapted for life in the trees. They have a prehensile tail that helps them anchor to branches and maneuver through the canopy. This unique adaptation allows them to remain perched on branches for long periods, waiting for prey to pass by.

3. **Hanging Technique**: Unlike many other snakes that coil around a branch, Green Tree Pythons use a distinctive hanging technique. They drape their body in a loop over a branch, allowing them to strike at prey from above.

4. **Slow Metabolism**: Green Tree Pythons have a relatively slow metabolism compared to some other snake species. This means they don't need to feed as frequently, which is advantageous given their arboreal lifestyle where prey might be less abundant.

5. **Docile Nature**: Despite their striking appearance, Green Tree Pythons are known for their generally calm and docile demeanor. This, along with their colorful patterns, makes them popular choices among reptile enthusiasts who are willing to provide the specialized care they require.

20. Hognose Snakes

These snakes are characterized by their distinct upturned snouts, which resemble a pig's snout. Hognose snakes are known for their intriguing behaviors and defensive tactics. When threatened, they often engage in dramatic displays such as spreading their necks, hissing loudly, and even playing dead by flipping onto their backs and opening their mouths.

Hognose snakes have a diverse range of habitats, including grasslands, woodlands, and sandy areas. They come in various species, with different color patterns and sizes. One well-known member of this group is the Eastern Hognose Snake (Heterodon platirhinos), which is often found in eastern and central North America. Despite their intimidating behaviors, hognose snakes are non-venomous and pose no serious threat to humans. They primarily feed on small prey like amphibians, toads, and rodents.

These snakes hold a special place in the hearts of reptile enthusiasts due to their unique appearance, fascinating behaviors, and harmless nature. They play an important ecological role by helping to control populations of certain pests and contributing to the overall biodiversity of North American ecosystems.

Fun Facts about Hognose Snakes:

1. **Upturned Snout:** The most distinctive feature of hognose snakes is their upturned snout, which gives them their name. This specialized snout helps them dig in loose soil and sand, aiding their burrowing behavior.

2. **Dramatic Defensive Tactics**: When threatened, hognose snakes are known for their elaborate defensive displays. These can include hissing, spreading their necks like a cobra, and even playing dead by flipping onto their backs and opening their mouths in a final attempt to deter predators.

3. **Variety of Species**: Hognose snakes belong to the genus *Heterodon* and encompass several species with different color patterns and sizes. For example, the Western Hognose Snake (*Heterodon nasicus*) features a more subdued color palette, while the Eastern Hognose Snake (*Heterodon platirhinos*) often has a striking pattern of dark blotches.

4. **Adaptive Habitats**: Hognose snakes are adaptable when it comes to habitats. They can be found in grasslands, woodlands, scrublands, and sandy areas. Their versatile diet and ability to burrow make them well-suited for different environments.

5. **Non-Venomous and Harmless**: Despite their sometimes dramatic behaviors, hognose snakes are non-venomous and pose no significant threat to humans. They primarily feed on small prey like toads, frogs, and rodents. Their elaborate displays are more about bluffing and deterring predators than causing harm.

21. Horned Vipers

Horned vipers, also known as horned adders, are a group of venomous vipers belonging to the genus Cerastes. These snakes are recognized for the distinctive pair of "horns" above their eyes, which are actually modified scales. These horn-like projections help break up their outline and aid in camouflage, making them harder to detect in their arid and sandy habitats.

Horned vipers are found in North Africa and the Middle East, often residing in deserts, semi-arid regions, and sandy dunes. They have a specialized burrowing behavior that allows them to partially bury themselves in the sand, with only their eyes and horns exposed, enabling them to ambush passing prey. Their venom is potent and is used to incapacitate their prey, which usually consists of small mammals, birds, and lizards.

Despite their venomous nature, horned vipers are generally not aggressive and prefer to rely on their cryptic coloration and ambush tactics to avoid confrontation. While they may not be as well-known as some other snake species, horned vipers play a crucial role in the ecosystems they inhabit by helping to control local prey populations.

Fun Facts about Horned Vipers:

1. **Horn-like Scales**: Horned vipers are named for the horn-like scales above their eyes. These scales, which are actually modified supraocular scales, help them blend into their sandy desert habitats by breaking up their outline and resembling small rocks or debris.

2. **Specialized Burrowing**: Horned vipers are skilled burrowers. They use their wedge-shaped heads and pointed snouts to dig into the sand, partially burying themselves while leaving only their eyes and horns exposed. This allows them to ambush prey that comes within striking distance.

3. **Camouflage Masters**: Their coloration and pattern are remarkably effective camouflage adaptations. Horned vipers often have shades of beige, brown, and gray that closely match the sand and rocks of their surroundings, making them nearly invisible to passing prey and potential predators.

4. **Nocturnal Lifestyle**: Horned vipers are primarily nocturnal, which means they are most active during the night. This behavior helps them avoid the extreme daytime temperatures of their arid habitats.

5. **Variety of Species**: The horned viper genus (*Cerastes*) includes several species, each with slight variations in appearance and range. For instance, the North African horned viper (*Cerastes vipera*) is known for its characteristic coloration and distribution across North Africa and the Middle East.

22. Indian Pythons

The Indian Python (Python molurus) is a large and powerful snake species native to the Indian subcontinent and parts of Southeast Asia. It is known for its impressive size, distinct pattern, and its role as one of the largest snake species in the world. Indian pythons are non-venomous constrictors, relying on their muscular bodies to capture and subdue prey.

These pythons can vary in color, ranging from light brown to olive or dark yellow, often displaying a series of dark blotches or patches along their bodies. Their scales are smooth and shiny, contributing to their striking appearance. Indian pythons are renowned for their ability to adapt to various habitats, from grasslands and marshes to forests and agricultural areas.

As ambush predators, Indian pythons hunt by concealing themselves and ambushing unsuspecting prey like rodents, birds, and small mammals. They are also known to occasionally prey on larger animals, using their powerful constriction technique to immobilize and consume their meals. Indian pythons play an essential ecological role in controlling prey populations, making them an integral part of their native ecosystems.

Fun Facts about Indian Pythons:

1. **Impressive Size**: Indian pythons are among the largest snake species in the world. They can reach lengths of up to 20 feet (6 meters) or even more. However, their size can vary based on factors such as habitat and available food.

2. **Constrictor Specialists**: Like all pythons, Indian pythons are constrictors. They capture their prey by coiling around it and

squeezing until it can no longer breathe. This powerful constriction technique helps them subdue and consume their meals.

3. **Variety of Habitats**: Indian pythons are incredibly adaptable and can be found in a range of environments, from grasslands and forests to agricultural areas and even near human settlements.

4. **Climbing Abilities**: Despite their large size and heavy build, Indian pythons are proficient climbers. They use their powerful muscles and sharp scales to move through trees and vegetation, which also aids them in capturing prey.

5. **Conservation Concerns**: Due to habitat loss, hunting for their skin and other body parts, and the exotic pet trade, Indian pythons are facing population declines and are considered a vulnerable species in many areas. Conservation efforts are underway to protect their populations and habitats.

23. Inland Taipans

The Inland Taipan (Oxyuranus microlepidotus), also known as the "fierce snake," holds the distinction of being the most venomous snake in the world. Native to the arid regions of Australia, particularly in Queensland, it possesses an incredibly potent venom that is capable of causing severe illness or death if not treated promptly. Despite its venomous nature, the Inland Taipan is quite reclusive and rarely encountered due to its remote habitat.

The Inland Taipan's coloration varies from light to dark shades of brown and olive, helping it blend into its arid surroundings. Despite its fierce reputation, this snake has a generally placid temperament and prefers to escape rather than confront threats. When it does deliver a bite, its venom contains a mix of neurotoxins and other components that can lead to rapid paralysis and other medical complications.

Conservation efforts are in place to protect the Inland Taipan's fragile population and preserve its unique role in the ecosystem. While it may not be as well-known as some other snake species, the Inland Taipan's record-breaking venom potency and role in the Australian ecosystem make it a species of interest among herpetologists and those fascinated by the world of reptiles.

Fun Facts about Inland Taipans:

1. **World's Most Venomous Snake**: The Inland Taipan holds the title of being the most venomous snake in the world. Its venom is incredibly potent, containing a mix of neurotoxins and other toxic components that can cause rapid paralysis and potentially fatal medical complications if not treated promptly.

2. **Reclusive Nature**: Despite its reputation, the Inland Taipan is quite reclusive and rarely encountered in the wild. It inhabits remote and arid regions of Australia, which contributes to its elusiveness.

3. **Cryptic Coloration**: The snake's coloration varies from pale to dark shades of brown and olive, allowing it to blend seamlessly into its desert habitat. This camouflage helps it remain hidden from both predators and prey.

4. **Non-Aggressive Demeanor**: Despite its potent venom, the Inland Taipan is generally non-aggressive and prefers to avoid confrontation. It relies on its cryptic coloration and tendency to flee when threatened.

5. **Small Population**: The Inland Taipan's population is relatively small, and its habitat is sensitive to disturbances. As a result, conservation efforts are in place to protect this unique snake species and its arid ecosystem.

24. King Cobras

The King Cobra (Ophiophagus hannah) is a highly venomous snake species and the longest venomous snake in the world. Found primarily in the forests and grasslands of Southeast Asia, the king cobra is known for its intimidating appearance, potent venom, and role as an apex predator. It gets its name from the distinctive hood it forms when threatened, which expands to make it appear larger and more menacing.

King cobras are skilled hunters that primarily feed on other snakes, including venomous ones. Their venom is a potent neurotoxin that targets the nervous system and can lead to paralysis and death if not treated promptly. Despite their venomous nature, king cobras are generally non-aggressive and prefer to avoid human interaction. When threatened, they can rear up a third of their body length and produce a distinctive hissing sound.

The king cobra's cultural significance and ecological role make it a subject of interest and respect in its native regions. It has inspired both awe and fear due to its size, unique behaviors, and formidable reputation as one of the most iconic and revered snakes in the world.

Fun Facts about King Cobras:

1. **Longest Venomous Snake**: The king cobra holds the distinction of being the longest venomous snake in the world. It can reach lengths of up to 18 feet (5.5 meters) or more, making it an imposing presence in its habitat.

2. **Apex Predator**: As an apex predator, the king cobra plays a vital role in its ecosystem by helping to control populations of other

snakes, including venomous ones. Its diet primarily consists of other snakes, but it also feeds on lizards, birds, and rodents.

3. **Venomous Threat Display**: When threatened, the king cobra is known for its iconic behavior of raising the front third of its body off the ground and spreading its distinctive hood to appear larger and more intimidating. It may also emit a loud hissing sound, which adds to the dramatic effect.

4. **Unique Diet**: While many snakes swallow their prey whole, the king cobra employs a different approach. It is known for its ability to eat other snakes, some of which can be quite large. The king cobra uses its strong jaws and flexible neck to maneuver and consume its meals.

5. **Cultural Significance**: The king cobra holds cultural significance in parts of its native range, particularly in India and Southeast Asia. It has often been featured in myths, religious stories, and local traditions, often as a symbol of power and reverence.

25. Mangrove Snakes

Mangrove snakes encompass a diverse group of snake species that are found in the mangrove ecosystems of tropical and subtropical regions around the world. These snakes are well adapted to the challenging and dynamic conditions of mangrove habitats, which include brackish water, mud, and tangled roots. Mangrove snakes are known for their specialized behaviors and appearances that enable them to thrive in these unique environments.

Mangrove snakes often have elongated bodies and flattened tails, adaptations that aid in swimming through the water and moving among the mangrove roots. Their coloration varies, but many species have patterns and colors that provide effective camouflage against the mangrove background. Some species of mangrove snakes are mildly venomous, using their venom to immobilize prey such as fish, frogs, and other small creatures.

Despite their adaptations to mangrove habitats, mangrove snakes can also be found in other environments, such as nearby forests or wetlands. They are efficient hunters and are particularly adept at capturing prey in the water, thanks to their streamlined bodies and ability to move through aquatic vegetation. These snakes play an important role in the mangrove ecosystem by helping to control populations of prey animals and contributing to the overall biodiversity of the area.

Fun Facts about Mangrove Snakes:

1. **Mangrove Specialists**: Mangrove snakes are well adapted to their unique habitat. Their streamlined bodies, flattened tails, and ability

to move through water and tangled roots make them skilled navigators in the challenging mangrove ecosystem.

2. **Variety of Species**: The term "mangrove snake" covers a range of species from different regions around the world. Each species has its own coloration and pattern adaptations that help it blend into its specific mangrove environment.

3. **Aquatic Abilities**: Many mangrove snake species are excellent swimmers. They use their bodies to glide through water and their tails to steer. This aquatic prowess is essential for hunting and finding shelter among the mangrove roots.

4. **Diurnal and Nocturnal**: While some mangrove snakes are primarily nocturnal, others are active during the day. This adaptability to different activity patterns helps them take advantage of various opportunities for finding food and avoiding predators.

5. **Viviparous Reproduction**: Some mangrove snake species give birth to live young, a reproductive strategy known as viviparity. This adaptation allows the young snakes to be born in or near the mangrove habitat, where they can immediately begin their lives in this unique ecosystem.

26. Paradise Flying Snakes

The Paradise Flying Snake (Chrysopelea paradisi) is a species of snake known for its remarkable gliding ability. Found in Southeast Asia, particularly in countries like Indonesia, Malaysia, and Thailand, this snake is a master of aerial locomotion and is often referred to as a "flying snake." Despite its name, it doesn't actually fly but rather uses a unique method of gliding through the air to move from tree to tree.

The Paradise Flying Snake's gliding ability is facilitated by its slender body and broad ventral scales. When it leaps from a tree branch, it flattens its body into a concave shape, which increases its surface area and creates an airfoil effect. The snake then undulates its body in a wave-like motion, allowing it to glide through the air for distances of up to 100 feet (30 meters) or more. This remarkable behavior helps it cover ground quickly and efficiently in its arboreal habitat.

Paradise Flying Snakes primarily feed on lizards and small mammals. They are non-venomous and harmless to humans. Their unique gliding behavior, cryptic coloration, and exceptional adaptability to their environment make them a fascinating and often studied species in the realm of herpetology.

Fun Facts about Paradise Flying Snakes:

1. **Aerial Gliders**: The Paradise Flying Snake is renowned for its exceptional gliding ability. It doesn't have wings or any true form of flight, but it uses its body shape and undulating movements to

glide skillfully through the air, moving between trees and covering impressive distances.

2. **Airfoil Adaptation**: When gliding, the snake flattens its body into a concave shape, resembling an airfoil. This shape, along with its lateral undulations, allows it to achieve controlled and relatively long glides, which is a unique adaptation for a snake species.

3. **Arboreal Lifestyle**: These snakes are highly arboreal, spending most of their time in trees. Their gliding behavior is a crucial adaptation for navigating through the forest canopy and accessing different parts of their habitat.

4. **Color Variation**: Paradise Flying Snakes exhibit a range of color variations, including shades of green, brown, and black. This coloration helps them blend into the foliage and remain concealed from both predators and prey.

5. **Swift Predators**: Paradise Flying Snakes are agile hunters. They primarily feed on lizards and small mammals. Their gliding ability allows them to swiftly move from one tree to another to search for prey and cover a large territory.

27. Reticulated Pythons

The Reticulated Python (Python reticulatus) is a massive and visually striking snake species found across Southeast Asia, including countries like Indonesia, Malaysia, and the Philippines. As one of the longest snake species in the world, the reticulated python can reach lengths of over 20 feet (6 meters) or more. Its name is derived from the intricate and beautiful reticulated pattern on its scales, which resembles a net-like mesh.

Reticulated pythons are constrictors, using their powerful bodies to wrap around and suffocate their prey. They have a diverse diet that includes mammals, birds, and sometimes even larger animals like deer and wild pigs. Due to their size, strength, and striking appearance, reticulated pythons have gained a mix of reverence and fear in the cultures where they are found.

While reticulated pythons are generally non-venomous and not considered a significant threat to humans, their large size and predatory nature make them important predators in their ecosystems. They play a crucial role in controlling prey populations and maintaining the balance of the food web in the tropical habitats they inhabit.

Fun Facts about Reticulated Pythons:

1. **Impressive Size**: Reticulated pythons are among the largest snake species in the world. They can reach lengths of over 20 feet (6 meters) and are known for their incredible size and strength. Some individuals have even been recorded at lengths exceeding 30 feet (9 meters).

2. **Distinctive Pattern**: The name "reticulated" comes from the intricate net-like pattern on their scales. Their beautiful and distinctive pattern provides excellent camouflage in their natural habitat of dense jungles and forests.

3. **Skilled Swimmers**: Reticulated pythons are excellent swimmers and are often found near water sources. They use their powerful bodies and strong muscles to navigate through water, making them effective hunters of aquatic prey.

4. **Varied Diet**: These pythons have a diverse diet that includes mammals, birds, and sometimes larger animals like deer and pigs. Their ability to consume such a wide range of prey contributes to their role as apex predators in their ecosystems.

5. **Reverence in Culture**: In some Southeast Asian cultures, reticulated pythons are both revered and feared. They hold a significant place in local folklore and beliefs, and their impressive size and reputation as powerful predators have contributed to their cultural significance.

28. Sidewinder Snakes

Sidewinder snakes is a term often used to describe a group of venomous vipers from North America that have a distinctive method of movement. One of the most well-known sidewinder species is the Mojave Desert sidewinder (Crotalus cerastes cerastes), which is found in the southwestern United States and northern Mexico. These snakes are specially adapted to thrive in the arid desert environments they inhabit.

Sidewinder snakes get their name from their unique method of locomotion. Instead of moving in a straight line like many other snakes, they move in a sideways or "sidewinding" manner. This movement helps them navigate through loose sand and prevents excessive body contact with the hot desert surface. By keeping only a few points of contact with the ground, they reduce friction and heat, making them more efficient in conserving energy and staying cool in their harsh habitat.

The sidewinder's ability to blend in with its desert surroundings, its sidewinding movement, and its venomous nature make it an intriguing and iconic species of snake in the southwestern United States and beyond.

Fun Facts about Sidewinder Snakes:

1. **Sidewinding Locomotion**: Sidewinder snakes are known for their unique method of movement called sidewinding. They move by pushing their bodies sideways and creating a series of J-shaped curves in the sand, which allows them to move efficiently across loose desert terrain without sinking into the sand.

2. **Specialized Adaptations**: Sidewinders have evolved several adaptations that make them well-suited for desert life. Their light coloration helps them blend into the sandy environment, and their upward-facing eyes assist in spotting prey and potential predators while their bodies remain partially buried in the sand.

3. **Efficient Heat Management**: Sidewinders use their sidewinding locomotion not only for efficient movement but also to manage their body temperature. By minimizing contact with the hot desert surface, they reduce heat absorption and stay cooler in the scorching environment.

4. **Venomous Predators**: Sidewinders are venomous vipers, and while their venom isn't as potent as some other viper species, it's still effective for subduing their prey. They primarily feed on small desert animals like rodents and lizards.

5. **Nocturnal Behavior**: Sidewinder snakes are primarily nocturnal, meaning they are most active during the cooler nighttime hours. This behavior helps them avoid the extreme daytime temperatures of their desert habitats.

29. Sunbeam Snakes

Sunbeam snakes refer to a group of non-venomous snakes found in various parts of Asia. One well-known species is the Burmese Sunbeam Snake (Xenopeltis unicolor), which is native to Southeast Asia. These snakes are named for their iridescent appearance, which gives them a shimmering quality when they catch the light. They are primarily ground-dwelling snakes, often found in forested areas and grasslands.

One of the striking features of sunbeam snakes is their glossy scales that reflect light like a prism, creating a play of colors that resembles a sunbeam. This iridescence is due to microscopic structures on their scales that refract and diffract light, resulting in a captivating display of colors. Sunbeam snakes are nocturnal and tend to be secretive, spending much of their time hidden in burrows or beneath debris.

Sunbeam snakes have adapted to a diet of small vertebrates, including rodents, frogs, and other small animals. Despite their somewhat cryptic lifestyle, their stunning appearance and unique adaptations have made them a favorite among snake enthusiasts who appreciate their subtle yet captivating beauty.

Fun Facts about Sunbeam Snakes:

1. **Iridescent Appearance**: Sunbeam snakes are known for their striking iridescence. Their scales reflect light in a way that creates a beautiful play of colors, giving them the appearance of a shimmering sunbeam. This unique feature sets them apart from many other snake species.

2. **Nocturnal Behavior**: Sunbeam snakes are primarily nocturnal, meaning they are most active during the night. This behavior allows them to avoid the heat of the day in their often tropical and humid habitats.

3. **Burrowing Habits**: These snakes are skilled burrowers and spend a significant amount of time underground. They create burrows or use existing ones for shelter and protection from predators and environmental conditions.

4. **Non-Venomous**: Sunbeam snakes are non-venomous and pose no threat to humans. Their main defense mechanism is to hide and avoid confrontation. When threatened, they might hiss or curl into a defensive posture.

5. **Unique Light Reflection**: The iridescence of sunbeam snakes is caused by structural colors, not pigments. Microscopic structures on their scales diffract and reflect light, creating the enchanting color display that sets them apart.

30. Threadsnakes

Threadsnakes, also known as wormsnakes or blind snakes, are a family of small and slender non-venomous snakes found in various parts of the world. These snakes are known for their diminutive size and inconspicuous appearance. Despite their unassuming nature, they play important roles in their ecosystems by preying on insects, termites, and other small invertebrates.

Threadsnakes are often mistaken for earthworms due to their small size, smooth and cylindrical bodies, and their habit of burrowing in the soil. They lack distinct eyes and have reduced vision, which suits their subterranean lifestyle. Threadsnakes have pointed snouts that help them burrow through the ground and locate their prey in the soil.

Some threadsnake species are parthenogenetic, meaning they can reproduce without fertilization by a male. They give birth to live young rather than laying eggs. Despite their unassuming appearance, threadsnakes are fascinating creatures that contribute to the balance of their ecosystems by controlling insect populations and playing a crucial role in nutrient cycling through their diet and behavior.

Fun Facts about Threadsnakes:

1. **Miniature Size**: Threadsnakes are some of the smallest snakes in the world, with some species reaching lengths of only a few inches. Their small size and slender bodies make them well-suited for their subterranean lifestyle.

2. **Elongated Bodies**: Threadsnakes have long, cylindrical bodies that resemble earthworms. This body shape allows them to navigate through tight spaces and burrows in the soil.

3. **Reduced Vision**: Threadsnakes often have reduced or even non-functional eyes due to their subterranean habits. Their reliance on senses like touch and smell helps them locate prey and navigate their underground habitats.

4. **Parthenogenesis**: Some threadsnake species are parthenogenetic, which means they can reproduce without mating with a male. This adaptation allows female snakes to produce offspring on their own.

5. **Cryptic Colors**: Threadsnakes often have plain and cryptic coloration that helps them blend into their underground environments. This camouflage helps them remain hidden from predators and ambushing prey.

31. Titanoboa

Titanoboa is an extinct genus of giant prehistoric snake that lived approximately 58 to 60 million years ago during the Paleocene epoch. It holds the distinction of being the largest snake ever known to exist, with estimates suggesting it reached lengths of up to 40 to 50 feet (12 to 15 meters) or even more. Fossils of Titanoboa were discovered in coal mines in Colombia, providing valuable insights into the ancient ecosystems of that time.

The discovery of Titanoboa has shed light on the climate and environment of the Paleocene era. Its immense size indicates a warm and tropical climate, which supported the growth of massive plant life and large prey animals. The snake likely preyed on large mammals and crocodile-like creatures that inhabited the waterways of its habitat.

Despite its impressive size, Titanoboa was not venomous. Instead, it would have used constriction to overpower its prey, much like modern-day anacondas and pythons. The discovery of Titanoboa has ignited scientific interest in understanding the evolutionary history of snakes and the factors that contribute to the development of such extraordinary sizes in certain lineages.

Fun Facts about Titanoboa:

1. **Gigantic Size:** Titanoboa holds the record for being the largest snake ever discovered. It reached incredible lengths of up to 40 to 50 feet (12 to 15 meters) or more, making it longer than a school bus. This massive size was possible due to the warm climate and abundance of large prey during the Paleocene epoch.

2. **Ancient Ancestor**: Titanoboa lived around 58 to 60 million years ago during the Paleocene epoch. Its discovery provides valuable insights into the ancient ecosystems and conditions that existed after the extinction of the dinosaurs.

3. **Fossil Evidence**: Fossils of Titanoboa were found in coal mines in the Cerrejón Formation in Colombia. The fossils include vertebrae, allowing scientists to estimate its size and reconstruct its appearance.

4. **Constrictor Lifestyle**: Despite its size, Titanoboa was not venomous like some modern large snakes. Instead, it relied on constriction to subdue its prey. Its powerful muscles and immense size would have allowed it to overpower even the largest of prey animals.

5. **Climate Clues**: The discovery of Titanoboa has provided important clues about the climate of its time. Its presence in tropical South America suggests that the region had a much warmer climate during the Paleocene epoch, supporting the growth of large plants and the evolution of massive animals.

MENTAL BOMB

Our goal is to entertain and to blow your mind!

Visit us online at MentalBomb.com
Home for the best illusions, riddles, games, and fun facts!

Follow

Facebook: Mental-Bomb-
Instagram: mental_bomb_
Pinterest: Mental_Bomb
Twitter: MentalBomb_